Correspondences With The Immortal

Correspondence with The Immortals

Letters & Poems

xxxxxxxx xxxxxxx xxxxxx

Edited with Commentary

J.L. Brewer

A catalogue of this book is available from the British Library

ISBN 9781909362871

Typeset in Helvetica and STSong

Editorial and Design by Kingston University MA Publishing Students:
Emma Chandler
Maddie Fagan
Jessica Oakes-Smith
Ollie Walter

KINGSTON UNIVERSITY PRESS
Kingston University
Penrhyn Road
Kingston-upon-Thames
KT1 2EE

Dedicated to

無心

for making this work possible.

To the Reader

East is East, West is West,
but the Other
always seems coolest.

Whatever you do,
beware of kanji tattoos—
they're a bitch to remove:

chicken soup, bitter idiot,
golden pig, coffin dude!

Even prize-winning poets
years after Pound
get the strokes wrong,
turn characters

upside-down.

For every step forward,
we moonwalk back
without ever knowing
what we lack.

Try if you can
to cut me some slack.

Contents

Part I
The Application

Part II
Off and Running!

Part III
A Sampling of Poems from
The Pavilion for Washing Away
Thoughts

.

Foreword

Quite recently, the world of Chinese scholarship was set astir when English translations of a few poems by an unknown poet named *Bao Wao* appeared on-line. It may be surprising to non-academics that anyone would have noticed stray specimens of a literary form that has long since had any real sway in our public discourse. To the uninitiated, it is hard to tell apart the sensitive detail in one Chinese poem from another. Nevertheless, there was something about the poems of *Bao Wao* that was both hauntingly familiar and fresh to the inner ears of the scholars who first spotted them. The content itself did not attract so much attention, but the translator—whoever he or she is—was given high marks for how natural *Bao Wao's* language sounded in English. Translations into other Western languages—French, Spanish, German, Slovenian etc.—quickly followed. All of them, however, were made directly from the English translation. You would think somebody would have taken the trouble to consult the original Chinese texts. I am not a Sinologist, but I have studied literature long enough to know how important it is when evaluating translations to go to the source. That seems elementary! Rather than wait for the criticism of *Bao Wao* to catch up, I took it upon myself to track down his original poems. I had no idea how difficult that would prove to be. I accessed the data banks of libraries here in the United States and around the world, not to mention in Beijing, Hong Kong, and Taipei, and came up empty. Of course, not all of the repositories of manuscripts have gone online. There also could be a bibliophile somewhere jealously guarding *Bao Wao's* original texts, just waiting for the market to increase their value. Will they turn up in the catalogue of a rare-book dealer, be put up for bids at an auction, listed on E-Bay, discovered in an attic or a garage sale? Who knows—I have spent many hours searching the Internet, googling "*Bao Wao*" and anything to do with him in a million different ways. Nothing!

Ah, but the simplest thing would be to go over his poems with a fine-tooth comb. Poets usually reveal themselves in subtle, yet obvious ways. Sure enough, my favorite poem "The Joy of Fishes," which takes place in the *Garden of Flowing Fragrance*, provides a key. The garden with its poetic-sounding name is an actual garden that exists outside of the poem in real time and real space, which you can pay money to visit any day of the week, except on Tuesday and special holidays. As the poem notes, "in this garden grow California oaks". Looking over their tops, you can view mountain ranges covered in California flora; the sky above is cloudless and Californian too. I wouldn't be surprised if you have already guessed this garden is the newest addition to the

Huntington Library's Botanical Gardens in San Marino, California (or "Chan" Marino as the non-pc locals say.) It is the pride of LA's well-heeled Chinese community, which is footing the multi-million-dollar bill for its construction. Imagine that—it's been only a century-and-a-half since the impoverished underclass of "long-tailed" immigrants risked their lives, blasting railroad-tunnels through the Sierras with sticks of dynamite, while their boss Collis P. Huntington, uncle of the library's founder, bought-off politicians in Washington. Lucky for me, in any case, I live in neighboring South Pasadena and, better yet, happen to know the former curator of the Huntington's Asian gardens, a delightful New Zealander, who wears a dapper Panama hat. From him, I have learned that the Chinese poet Zhang Longxi came to the Huntington in 2015 and wrote four traditional poems to commemorate the *Garden of Flowing Fragrance*, which my friend faithfully translated into English as "fluent and proficient" as the original Chinese.

The first thing you will note is how scholarly they are. The poet cannot help but call attention to the famous literary topos of Tao Yuanming's "Peach Blossom Spring," a rhetorical gesture that I feel comes between himself and the actual garden. In fact, the concluding lines of the final poem ask us to "reverently salute Yuanming's integrity," which might appeal to a fellow academic, but to quote Allen Ginsberg— "allegories are so much lettuce." Casual visitors could care less about an old poet they will never read. Believe me, the Huntington's Chinese Garden with its exotic pavilions, stone bridges, and lotus filled pond can speak for itself. *Bao Wao's* poem is more of a "reality sandwich" and less burdened by his debt to the canon of Chinese poetry and its formal rules of composition. He doesn't have to restrict himself to octaves of five characters per/line or—God forbid—expend energy looking up puns in the Qing Dynasty dictionary, *Poetic Rhymes from the Hall of Honoring Literature.* True, "The Joy of Fishes" tips its hat to tradition—the last line comes from Chuang Tzu—but it is not nostalgic. The immediacy of *Bao Wao's* experience in the *Pavilion for Washing Away Thoughts* allows us to enter into his mind. We, too, can feel what both he and Chuang Tzu felt as they realized the joy of fishes was no different than their own joy!

You can track down Zhang Longxi through the Yenching Institute at Harvard, but there is nothing in his poetic DNA to suggest he is *Bao Wao* or that he would be acquainted with a virtually anonymous poet who took the "not taken road" —i.e. the road that leads away from literary success. The person best positioned to identify *Bao Wao* is the former curator who inspected the garden he oversaw every day. Surely, he would not have passed-up a chance to engage with a sensitive-looking East-Asian man, sitting in the *Pavilion for Washing Away Thoughts* with a brush and notebook in hand. Unfortunately, my friend abruptly quit his plum position two winters ago and returned to New Zealand. I don't believe he has anything to hide, but I am still waiting for an answer from the last e-mail I sent him. In any case, I suspect that "The Joy of Fishes" was written sometime after he left.

I would speculate further that it was written on a Tuesday when the garden is closed to the public. You will note *Bao Wao* says in the poem that [his] ears are the only ears being washed by the sound of the falls. Actually, that is a bit hyperbolic because on Tuesday there are also gardeners walking about performing their gardening duties—hand watering, mowing lawns, pruning trees, and tending roses next to the English Tea Room. More to the point, there are registered Readers from the library who occasionally take breaks from their research and stroll through the picturesque Japanese and Chinese gardens. If you want to find *Bao Wao*, you would do well to look amongst this group of scholars. Of course, all of them have or are working towards a Ph.D., but the library, unless it is handing out grant money, does not keep tabs on how serious they really are about their research. The truth is there are so many over-achieving academics around the world who flock to the collections that the Huntington's reputation will not suffer in the slightest if one of them turns out to be a "do-nothing" poet who has no intention of being cooped up in the rare-book room, rooting through the past for that precious nugget of information, which would help him put to bed some issue that—lo and behold—he alone has just discovered is "problematic." Trust me, he would head straight for the *Pavilion for Washing Away Thoughts*, where he could chill, breath deep, and "take delight in water," just as every Chinese sage has done since Confucius first said in the *Analects* that this is what wisemen do.

Well, only a few weeks ago I went to the Huntington myself on a Tuesday. Before the library opened its doors, I sat outside on a bench in a nook reading the New York Times on my laptop. On the other side of a bush blocking my view, I heard one of the volunteer waterers talking to someone as she watered a large pot of succulents. I wasn't bothering to listen in on everything they were saying, but I picked up on the friendliness of their conversation just like Frost catching "the sound of sense" on the other side of one of his walls. But then a phrase leapt to my ear— "Oh, *Wao* I would really like to read those poems someday." You can imagine how my ears pricked up. I was burning to see for myself if this could be the author of those texts I had been trying so hard to track down. After the watering-lady finished her watering and went on to the next group of pots, I stood up, took a few noiseless steps to the path, turned to my right, and as I passed by, I tried to glance casually at whoever had been talking to her. Expecting to see a

Chinese man of no-determinate age, I spied instead a typical-looking American academic about seventy years old—trim, bearded, with thinning grey hair, wearing, as you would expect, wire-rim glasses. Confused and not wanting to stare, I continued on down the path and took refuge in the reading room of the library.

In time, I was able to collect my thoughts and came to the obvious conclusion that the name *Bao Wao* could be a pseudonym for a writer who may or may not be Chinese! Lots of Westerners "go native" and become fluent in Asian languages. Lafcadio Hearn, who married a samurai's daughter, is only known in Japan by his adopted name, Koizumi Yakumo. I believed the watering-lady talking to *Bao Wao* was being charmingly familiar when she addressed the poet on the bench with his Chinese given-name. Why not? In any case, I considered if he was friendly enough to strike up a casual relationship with her, he would probably be willing to talk to me too. I hurried out of the library and went straight to the bench where he had been sitting, but of course he wasn't there, nor was he to be found anywhere else in the Huntington's 240 acres of buildings and grounds. I made the whole grand-tour feeling like the boy in Master Kusan's picture-book about catching the Bull. It has been years since I looked at the ten chapters of that pithy Zen fable, but I immediately returned home and took down from the shelf my old copy of *Zen Flesh-Zen* Bones and perused it again.

Chapter One announces the search for the Bull. In Chapter Two, the Bull's footprints are spotted, and in Chapter Three, the Bull itself is seen for the first time. This, in effect, is the stage I had reached in my search. True, I had no objective confirmation that the man on the bench was Bao Wao, nor of course had I seen any of the Chinese versions of the poems themselves, but I had caught a glimpse—metaphorically speaking—of his head and horns. Having arrived at this stage, then surely Chapters Four, Five, and Six, which describe capturing the Bull, taming it, and riding it back home were not far behind. This was highly encouraging. The plot seemed ineluctable, pre-determined, but this, in turn, got me to thinking about the last four chapters. What to make of the idea in Chapter Seven that the Bull is transcended and, hence, no longer exists for its herder? Even more challenging is the idea in Chapter Eight that his own self is transcended too. The accompanying illustration, true to Zen iconography, is an empty circle—no Bull, no boy, no hut, no trees, no sun, no moon! How foolish I felt to be locked into the pursuit of the very thing I would ultimately leave behind. The Nothing I started with and the Nothing of this stage seemed to be equal. Then I turned the page and came to Chapter Nine illustrated with the image of a flowering-tree dropping petals into a flowing brook. Something clicked, as I read the title— "Reaching the Source." Of course, it occurred to me that this must be "Peach Blossom Spring," which the Harvard poet alludes to in his formal poems about the garden.

What a coincidence! Everything, I was forced to admit, seemed to point in the direction of Tao Yuanming's enduring fable. To refresh your memory of its plot— a humble fisherman, during a period of political instability, inadvertently paddles up a blossom-strewn river that ends in a grotto, where he squeezes through a narrow passageway that opens into an idyllic land, utterly free of normal human strife. I figured the Eight Immortals, those remarkable T'ang Dynasty literati known for the timeless world they created for themselves through the miraculous power of their poetry (and wine) most likely hang out there, too. I didn't imagine myself literally traveling up that same river in a boat in order to reach them, but I understood I needed to make contact by other means if I wanted to "reach the source" and with their help solve the mystery of *Bao Wao*. I remembered how James Merrill—brilliant gay-poet son of the famous financier—wrote a five-hundred-page epic-length poem about his one thousand nights at the Ouija board. Only a genius like Merrill could get away with being so indefatigably arch. I wouldn't be caught dead taking such a hokey parlor game as seriously as he apparently did. I resolved, instead, to access my inner-google without relying on any intervening hardware, neither computer nor Ouija board. It took a while to get the hang of it, but when I did the results were far more rewarding than my outer-google search to unearth *Bao Wao's* Chinese texts.

How gratifying it was to get a direct response to my purely mental queries! As quick as thought itself, I heard from *J'Han-shan*, the spokesperson for the Eight Immortals. He expressed surprise that I was able to contact them. Hard to believe, but it seems that in the last thousand years or so there has been only one other person besides myself who has successfully established a line of communication with this august group of scholars. Both of us, it turns out, have the same ethnicity, the same educational background, are the same age, and live in the same period. I was doubly amazed when I learned that the Other has, at least, three aliases besides *Bao Wao*. Most surprising, is the pseudonym xxxxxxxx xxxxxxx xxxxxx, a deliberate obfuscation, I suspect, of his birth name. How the plot thickens! At a glance, I could tell those three sets of x's make up the same number and pattern of letters in the pen name I recently adopted in an effort to protect my somewhat fragile ego. I literally turned dizzy at the realization I might have accidentally stumbled upon my very own doppelgänger. After I expressed my confusion to the Immortals, they thoughtfully filled me in on their side of the story.

Out of the blue, just a short time ago, they received a formal letter from xxxxxxxx xxxxxxx xxxxxx. I can attest from my own experience that the Immortals are so well-known that he didn't need to designate their address. His strong intention to engage with them was all it took for his communique to land in their hands. While they scratched their heads and tried to figure out who had sent it and how it had reached them, xxxxxxxx xxxxxxx xxxxxx fired off five more follow-up letters. Only then did the Immortals send back their somewhat indignant response. As you can imagine, xxxxxxxx xxxxxxx xxxxxx was amazed to have heard from them, as well as he should have been, since rather cavalierly, if you ask me, he hadn't bothered to provide a return address. Of course, he replied immediately—that would be his seventh letter if you are keeping track—and the correspondence continued on its merry way. Who knows if it will ever end? The Immortals, I am proud to say, passed on to me every communication exchanged so far. They declared the public had the right to know the history of their relationship with the poet who most recently has gone by the name *Bao Wao.* You can now read all of the correspondence painstakingly transcribed from my inner mind, letter by letter, as though I were following the pointer on a Ouija board.

I don't want to let the cat out of the bag and spoil your readerly enjoyment of the story you are about to see unfold, but I do want to give a heads-up. In the first letter xxxxxxxx xxxxxxx xxxxxx sends to the Immortals, you will learn about his scheme to become recognized as a poet. However outlandish it may seem to you at first,

I hope in time you will come to sympathize with him, perhaps, even respect him, regardless of your opinion of his poetry. Think of it this way—how many people do you know who have successfully initiated and carried-on a lively correspondence with the Eight Immortals! Need I declare what a great accomplishment that is? If you are as curious as I am, you will want to decipher xxxxxxxx xxxxxxx xxxxxx's name. Of course, I have a few good hunches about what those twenty-one place-holders are hiding, but I don't presume his x's cover-up the same letters my y's cover up. Sooner or later, I suspect, some dedicated researcher at the Huntington will beat everyone to the punch and disclose the "real names" for scholars to bandy about in one of those "Brown Bag Talks" that are open to the registered Readers at lunch time. Just picture me sitting at the back of the room, waiting for the big reveal—how mixed my emotions will be!

—yyyyyyyy yyyyyyy yyyyyy
c/o The Huntington Library, Art Collections,
& Botanical Gardens
San Marino, California—August 4, _____

I

The Application

You sit around saying:
We are unknown, if someone
should recognize you, what would you do?

—Analects, Bk. XI, Ch. XXV

The First Letter

Dear Immortals (wherever you may reside):

I would like to apply to become a Chinese poet.
This may seem odd to you since I do not claim to be Chinese,
nor do I even speak, read, or write Chinese.

I have, though, been reading Chinese poetry in English
since I was a teenager.
I believe my lack of Chinese should not disqualify me
from joining the ranks of poets
whom I have admired for so long.

Please understand, I have no ambition to be
a Chinese-Chinese Poet
skilled in your traditional techniques.
I am seeking to become a Translated-Chinese Poet,
who is read in free-verse English only.

Poets, usually, are not translated unless already
considered famous, but I am making the case
that a heretofore unknown poet
may be worthy of this honor. Need I suggest—
since the original language and the target language
are one and the same, the translations
are guaranteed to be perfectly faithful.

That's good for both of us—none of the "poetry" of the poetry will be lost!

Sincerely Yours,

xxxxxxxx xxxxxxx xxxxxx

P.S. Since I have already "translated" my poems (if you get my drift), there's no need to pay someone else to do the job.

First Follow-Up Letter

Dear Immortals
(I trust you guys read English, too):

By now you have had the opportunity to review
my previous letter in which I announced
my desire to become a Translated-Chinese Poet.
My intention was to break the ice—stir your interest!
Now let me get down to business and detail
the many ways I think you will consider me
a sympathetic applicant.

I come from a proud if not wealthy family.
Its genealogy can be traced back to the founding
of our nation, the time of our Yao and Shun.
My male ancestors, up through the last century,
have served as officers in every one of our major
armed conflicts, both on the continent and overseas.
Named after the family's first hero,
wounded at Bunker Hill, I am the last in line
(with no living offspring).
When my time came to support a war,
I followed, instead, the Buddha's precept, "Not to kill."

I grew up in a house with a good library.
I especially prize the books my mother passed on to me—

four pocket-size volumes of Shelley's poetry,
a Roycroft edition of Emerson's *Nature,*
and *Buena Vista Windows,* a book of verses
written by her grandaunt Jane Lippitt Patterson,
editor of *The Christian Leader* and ardent Abolitionist.
O what a high-minded legacy!

On my father's side, three generations of surgeons
preceded me. He told me— "You can become
anything you want just as long as you serve Mankind."
Too much of a "do-nothing" to study biology and
chemistry, I read poems instead,
attracted to Orientalists like Yeats, Pound, and Snyder.
Inadvertently, I was laying the ground to become
one of those introverted doctors
who don't wield scalpels but write dissertations
only a committee of three will ever see.
I don't expect you to read mine, but the title alone,
Closing the Circle: Eastern Visions in Western Verse,
will bolster your faith in my application.

I am well-traveled by all means of human conveyance
over land and water. I often fly through the air, too!
These days you can do that without being a *sennin.*
I know the Landscape of Mountains and Rivers,
and in my youth, I rode horseback through a wilderness
as cold and remote as Han-shan's Cold Mountain.

I have soaked up the culture of capital cities,
watched splendid Imperial processions, burned incense
in shrines, sipped tea in teahouses, strolled Suzhou gardens,
watched "Farewell My Concubine," and attended exhibitions
of calligraphy and ink-brush paintings. I don't claim
to be a connoisseur of the "Four Major Cuisines,"
but I never leave a grain of rice in my rice bowl,
and I am dexterous enough to pick up three oily peanuts,
side by side, with my chopsticks, all at the same time
without dropping them—try it!

My generation has been stamped by more
than one seismic cultural shift, due to the ongoing
aftershocks of our own An Lu Shan Rebellion.
To this day, the country is still divided
between White and Black, Red and Blue,
and—dare I say—Smart and Dumb.
I am used to being at odds with my government's policies
and those of other regimes 'round the world, too.
I lived as an ex-pat for twenty-five years,
earning my keep as a Foreign Lecturer of Literature
moving from city to city, country to country,
far from my native home.

During the first chapters of our "floating life,"
my younger wife and I alighted like birds
in tiny apartments with six-mat rooms,

sweating concrete walls, patched shoji screens
and mildewed closets. We counted ourselves lucky
when our rent was subsidized,
and we could look through the borrowed
scenery of neighboring rooftops
and spot the peak of a sacred mountain.

Recently retired, I now half-own a leaf-shadowed house
that needs to be repaired and repainted.
I feel burdened by the stuff my parents left behind—
old furniture, artwork, knick-knacks,
and file cabinets filled with letters, bills, and documents.
Each item, down to the last scrap of paper has a history
and is imbued with sentiment.

My wife and I sleep in the same tester bed
my father and mother slept in.
We dine alone each night at the same fine table
I ate at as a child. All of our friends,
scattered far and wide, seem like phantoms.
Days go by when we don't meet anyone else.
Without servants, we perform our menial chores best
as we can, ignoring the daily slide into *wabi-sabi.*
It's all I can do to keep up with falling leaves—
you tell me how the garden can be overgrown
and dying at the same time!

Meanwhile, my hair is thinning, eyes drying, teeth
yellowing. Knees are gimpy, fingers achy.
And memory takes longer and longer to download.
Proper nouns go on walkabouts for hours on end
before they stroll back and greet me again.

When I was younger, I meditated in Hsüan-tsang's
promised land. I didn't reach there by trekking
across the Gobi Desert and the Hindu Kush,
but for nearly ten years, I got up every morning
before dawn and struggled to reduce
my thoughts to one thought only.
After my guru died (in the nick of time,
before his indictable behavior was exposed),
I swung the other way, working hard to cram
my mind with knowledge for the sake of a career.

Now I am going to idle away the hours in my idyll,
maybe even finish all four volumes of
Journey to The West. Rest assured; I'll be ready
when called upon to shift into
high gear and sing my own "swan-song."

Sincerely Yours,

xxxxxxxx xxxxxxx xxxxxx

Second Follow-Up Letter

Dear Immortals
(you might want to check out Fed-Ex):

I have been thinking over my last letter
in which I listed what I believe are my strong points.
Like most applicants, I may have erred
in tooting my own horn just a little too loud.
Here I want to tackle a few reservations you might have
in considering me as a candidate.

I must confess unlike many of your poets, I've never
been awarded (or demoted) with a sinecure
as a low-level magistrate.
This is not to say I haven't had my share
of soul-damaging, futile work.
Three decades of teaching composition would drive
just about anybody with an educated mind
into the alluring arms of self-indulgence
or, at least, cause a mild case of PTSD.

I hope it will not go against me that I have
lived abstemiously throughout my life
and have no interest in getting drunk.
A Quietist at heart, I often fantasize building
a thatched hut next to a mountain-monastery

just like Bai Juyi. Take my word—sooner or later
someone will declare which of my poems
is my *enlightenment poem.* Then you'll forgive me
for not exaggerating the virtues of an artificial high
induced by one of those deadly clear liquors
you'd never guess could be distilled from such
honorable staples as sorghum or rice.
Conviviality in itself is laudable,
but who wants to get soused with a bunch
of sloppy bros or much worse all alone?

So be it, if I sound too moralistic for your taste.
Immortals have never heard of alcohol abuse, A.A.
or co-dependency. Your Mothers
never banded against Drunk Driving!

Sincerely Yours,

xxxxxxxx xxxxxxx xxxxxx

Third Follow-Up Letter

Dear Immortals
(don't forget to send back the proof of delivery form):

Three straight letters, I realize, is a lot to ask you to read.
Oh, but there are so many issues we need to discuss
if our project (assuming you accept) is going
to be a success. Perhaps, you are wondering where
you could situate me in the lineage of Chinese poets.
I don't expect to be included alongside
such luminaries as Li Bai or Tu Fu.
A more modest period than the Tang,
even the debased present will do just fine.

Biographical details can be kept to a minimum.
My work, I feel, stands on its own
and needs little contextualization.
What is most important is that the readers
who pick up my book will be confident
they are holding translations of poems
written by a Chinese poet.
I can assure you my themes will be
traditional Chinese themes:
moon-viewing, gazing upon mountain peaks,
bemoaning personal misfortune,
lamenting the state of the nation.

The philosophically inclined will never suspect
I was raised in the West;
far from being Cartesian, my stance
is scrupulously non-dualistic.
Literary critics, too, will happily identify
that indispensable hallmark of lyrics
inspired by the *Shih-ching*—
"have no twisty thoughts."

I can't over-stress how eager I am to get started!
This is just the shot in the arm my career
as an unread author needs.
It would be so much better to be an actual
Chinese poet, rather than a warmed-over Imagist
trying to match the clarity and depth
of Classical Chinese Poetry.

As for my new name, may it sound
authentic—be easy to pronounce.

Sincerely Yours,

xxxxxxxx xxxxxxx xxxxxx

Fourth Follow-Up Letter

Dear Immortals
(by the way, I forgot to ask if you FaceTime or Skype):

Let me get straight to the point.
I realize Time doesn't exist for you,
but it sure does for me.
Please understand I am not getting any younger.
I would deeply appreciate an answer as soon as possible.
I only recently conceived of my scheme,
but I think it will be a win-win for everybody.
I will earn the recognition I deserve,
and the tradition of Chinese poetry
will be able to add one more poet—albeit a minor one—
to its three-thousand-year-old canon.

It's my impression that poetry these days has
become increasingly
unpopular and marginalized.
I suspect the brutal Great Leaps Forward
under Mao Tse Tung
has something to do with its decline.
Who cares if he had talent as a poet—
his Cultural War on the Old Ways
was an unmitigated disaster.
No question, as guardians of poetry

you would be more trusted
if you kicked out a moral monster
from your anthologies
and welcomed a pacifist like myself,
even if I am illiterate in Chinese.

I am afraid you will have to handle
the poetic labor-market in your country
the same way we turn a blind eye on migrant workers
sneaking across the border to do the work
that citizens don't want to do.
I am happy, though, to toil in the vineyards of poetry
for no more recompense than your recognition
that I am a Translated Chinese poet.
Sure, it would be sign of good faith if you could throw in
a tin of jasmine tea, plus a black embroidered hat
(the kind formerly worn by Taoist masters),
but I won't insist upon it.

Your choices, I believe, are becoming
increasingly limited. Given
the strides your techies have made in A.I.,
you could hand over the writing of poetry to robots.
Or, more realistically, you can outsource
your precious tradition to eager humans like myself
who will keep the heart of poetry alive.

Never forget, when you're talking Literature—
"Only emotion endures."

Sincerely Yours,

xxxxxxxx xxxxxxx xxxxxx

Envoy

Dear Immortals
(is climate change slowing your mail-service?)

Silent though you have been ever since
I first wrote to you, I just want you to know
with each successive letter I have sent
I believe we have grown closer together.
I felt, at first, as bashful as the fourteen-year-old bride
in the Li Bai poem famously translated by Fenollosa
and that "difficult individual," Ezra Pound.
Do you remember (of course, you remember—
your founder wrote it!) At fifteen
she stopped scowling and desired her dust
to be mingled with her young husband's dust.
At sixteen, he went away on a business trip,
and she suffered greatly in his absence.
The monkeys' cries in the trees became sorrowful;
the sight of the paired yellow butterflies
in the West Garden hurt her!
Not that we have any familial bonds,
but when you finally choose to answer my letters
I have this to say to your Heavenly courier:

If you are coming down through the narrows
of the river Kiang, please let me know

beforehand, and I will come out to meet you
as far as Chō-fū-Sa.

(And not one step further!)

Faithfully Yours,

xxxxxxxx xxxxxxx xxxxxx

II

Off and Running!

To chop an axe-handle, to chop an axe-handle.
The model is not far.

—Book of Songs, #158

A Surprise Reply

To xxxxxxxx xxxxxxx xxxxxx
(wherever you may reside):

We understand that it is customary
for human institutions to thank applicants
who are applying for particular positions,
but the sheer impertinence of your unsolicited letters
has given us pause.

How you managed to reach us is a mystery,
even to us who are well-versed
in the esoteric practices of Taoism.
At first, we were dead set against any sort of reply,
written or otherwise.
Then you didn't let up and continued to barrage us.
Six letters in all by our count!

We finally called an emergency get together
to decide as a group what to do.
Lucky for you, after several rounds of toasts
to our own good sense,
the silliness of your proposal began to tickle
our imaginations.
If our founder Li Bai could earn everlasting fame
by doing something so stupid as trying

to embrace the moon's reflection in a lake,
then an argument can be made
for rewarding your delusion too.
Indeed, given the dim prospects in your native place,
you could do worse than seek
our acceptance of you as a Chinese poet.

Don't expect us, though, to act as your literary agents!
When it comes to finding a publisher
and hashing out a contract, you are on your own.
Perhaps, if you were a little less uptight
and spent more time schmoozing at wine parties
like we did when forging our reputations
you might make some helpful contacts.

Be that as it may, we want to impress
upon you that the Immortals in our band
are like those lilies in foreign fields.
Far be it from us to toil and spin!
The only thing we are willing to do for you
is come up with a name
that will sound sufficiently Chinese
for the non-native Chinese readers
you're trying to reach.
Now that is a linguistic challenge
we can still take some interest in.

Believe us, we had quite a rowdy session
trying to pick an appropriate pseudonym for you.
Immortal Poet after Poet shouted out
one idea after another.
It's been many dynasties since our creative juices
flowed so freely. We wondered
how to choose from such an embarrassment
of riches, but choose we did—a name,
we think, that suits you to a Tea
and, at the same time, echoes our tradition.

Let it be official: henceforth, you will be known to us
and the world as **Rong Wei.**

I have the honor to speak for the Eight Immortals,

J'Han-shan
Peach Blossom Spring
Somewhere near Wu Ling

The Correspondence Continues

c/o J' Han-shan
Peach Blossom Spring
Somewhere near Wu Ling

Dear Immortals (*voila!*):

Imagine what a dizzy tailspin you sent me into
just by answering my unsolicited application
to be a Translated-Chinese Poet.
Boundless gratitude is what I first felt
before I even opened your communication.

Breathlessly skimming your precious lines,
my eyes leapt to the last sentence
that proclaimed my new name—*Rong Wei.*
Eager as I was, I couldn't help but hear
in my mind *Wang Wei.*

 Then presto, just as you would expect,
I pictured the scene of his most famous short poem
as though I had written it myself!

Deer Park

Empty mountain—no one seen,
yet voices echo in the wood.
Shafts of the setting sun light up
green moss on rocks, in trees.

How remarkable is this quatrain—there seems to be
nothing personal here.
No emotion we could attach to the poet,
no view that he claims for himself.
Yet the poem didn't just spring up on the mountainside.
It has been sneakily titled
with a reference to the grove where the Buddha taught,
then stamped with the poet's own seal.

What a paradox—by realizing the truth of Emptiness
in himself and creation,
Brother Wei becomes a universally known personage—
not bad for one who supposedly lost his ego!

There's a lesson for me to learn here,
but as fate would have it,
later in the day after your letter came,
I was driving along Bellefontaine Street,
planning to make a turn onto St. John Avenue;
I slowed down, looked to my right,

and read— **"Wrong Way—Do Not Enter."**
Only then did I realize you had played me for a fool.
No wonder you had such a high old time
at my naming party.

Oh, poets are a tricky lot. Immortal poets
the trickiest of them all!
Shall I take a hint and swallow my pride?
Li Bai himself encountered plenty
of "Do Not Enter" signs,
until he was redeemed and joined your select few.
My aim, though, is far more modest.
I am not seeking membership
in your Immortal drinking club.
I'd be satisfied with the lesser kind of Immortality
dished out in sonnets, which nobody takes too seriously.
Please do better, though, than that old chestnut #18
which promises eternal life for its sunny addressee
without even naming him.
No, skin off Shakespeare's back, hey?

Ok, I am still chewing on my Rongness.
It would be nice at the moment
if you could show a little compassion.
Dare I mention Kuan Yin?
Come to think of it, where in your poetry
do you invoke "The Goddess of Mercy"?

At least, Li Bai has adopted sympathetic
female personae. That shows his Great-Heartedness.
When it comes down to it, I bet most of you
are more attached to the Lesser Vehicle than you let on.
If you are going to be such sticklers,
please tell me how I have strayed from the Path.
Which of those Rights have I wronged?
Has my View failed to be Right?
Do I not have Right Resolve, Right Effort?
My Speech may seem to be more Left than Right,
but my Livelihood has to be Right
given how little I have ever been paid!
As for Right Mindfulness and Right Samadhi
(the most difficult of all),
I am now putting my Right Foot forward.
You can rest assured
my mostly Right Conduct
will get me enlightened sooner or later.

My sympathies, in any case, are as much Taoist
as they are Buddhist or Confucian.
I admire the way Lao Tzu favors *weak* over *strong,*
dark over *bright, soft* over *hard,*
water over *stone*—in short, *yin* over *yang.*
If I remember correctly didn't he also say—
"The *W-e-i* that can be named is not the *W-e-i*"?

Just kidding! You can tell how much I am smarting
about my new name. I warn you
once you start hearing puns it's hard to stop.
Take the surname *Wang*, which you mockingly
withheld from me. It may mean "king" in Chinese,
but surprise! the same sound signifies
something very different in the native slang
of my democratic homeland.
I am loathe to spell out a vulgarity,
yet truth be told like many men I know
I'd rather be called "Wrong" than a **"D-i-c-k."**

I remain,

xxxxxxxx xxxxxxx xxxxxx

The Bestowal of a Second Name

Dear Mr. Pissy Pants
(aka *Rong Wei*):

O ignorant man you should think twice about
starting a pissing war with us.
From our Heavenly Abode, we can rain down
buckets of pee upon your silly head
before you'll ever piss up.

God, how tedious you are.
There's a famous book, we hear, called Job
which describes the likes of you.
Kvetch, kvetch, kvetch···is that the word we want?
You should be glad we responded to your
application with gentle ribbing
and didn't bully you with a whirlwind.

Look, we understand you couldn't handle the truth
and tried to send you a message via a dumb pun,
but you got all huffy and fired back with
one of your own. Your problem is that
you are now over seventy years old
and still think the world owes you something.

Get a grip, man—if you were good enough
to be considered a "Chinese Poet In Translation,"
you would be good enough to be published
in your native language.
Is it any wonder that we chose to call you
"Wrong Way"?
The truth is your whole scheme is an obvious scam.
You know fully well that anyone who reads
translations assumes they're better
in the original language.
That works for you as long as someone
who knows Chinese doesn't ask to see
the original texts of your poems.

Speaking of which, when are you going to send us
some samples of your work?
Let's hope they are more lively than those filler poems
readers flip past each week in *The New Yorker*
on the way to the next cartoon.
The language of these poetasters' verse is so affected
it has about as much chance
of soaring up to our Heavenly Realm
as a dodo bird on a pair of vestigial wings.

Of course, just because wings no longer work as wings
doesn't mean you can't fantasize about flying.
We'll give you credit on that score,

no matter how impossible your dream may be.
We'll commend you, too, for turning to our tradition
in your desperation, given that it would've
been more plausible for you to reinvent yourself
as a poet fluent in one of those tongues
that rose from the ashes of Vulgar Latin.
But, no, you chose us because of the human scale
of our poets' subject matter
and the freshness of their expression.
Your appreciation alone has led us to reconsider
our response. Sure, you try our patience,
but at the end of the day you don't deserve
to be called "Mr. Pissy Pants" or *Rong Wei*.

Last night, we had another rousing drinking fest
and bandied about a whole slew of new names for you.
We are pleased to say our final choice was unanimous.
Henceforth, may you be called **Qi Ho-tei**.
Now go forth and slay those giant windmills,
and above all win your Lady's respect!

I have the honor to speak for the Eight Immortals,

J' Han-shan
Peach Blossom Spring
Somewhere near Wu Ling

A Springboard to Immortality

c/o J' Han-shan
Peach Blossom Spring
Somewhere near Wu Ling

Dear Immortals (sigh):

Here we go again. Out of the wok into the fire,
one way or another my goose is going to get cooked.
Rong Wei was downright humiliating,
but *Qi Ho-tei* is hardly better.

My native English speaking audience has ears too.
Unless you are a mono-lingual Brit who believes
the deluded Don's name is pronounced *"Kwik-sit,"*
you can't help but hear "Quixote" in *Qi Ho-tei.*

For the second time, you have undone
my credibility with a pun.
I imagine you are chuckling over the possibility
that I will be known, henceforth,
as "Man of La Manchukuo"
How sly you are! Only non-Chinese people,
the imperialistic Japanese, to be precise,
are comfortable using that name.

Please give me one good reason why I would
like to be saddled with the historical
baggage of an infamous period.
I am not seeking to be read by a Chinese audience,
but I don't want my English readers to doubt
the Chinese-ness of my translated poems,
especially since they may know I lived and worked
beyond the Yellow Sea in the very same nation
that pulled the strings of The Last Emperor.

I wonder how much more mockery I can take?
I suspect you Lucys will always whip away
the proverbial football from my eager foot,
I keep going in circles— love me/love me not,
but how can I resist the one in a million chance
that I will receive your stamp of approval?

And besides you have mercifully refrained from
raining down pee on my head.
What the hell, call me *Qi-Ho-tei* if it amuses you.
I fully expect you will make jokes about me
mounting my *Russian Auntie*···. "Look, there he goes
clip-clopping across those plains where it seldom rains
with that fatso *Sansho Ponzu!* in tow."

I only ask that you do not insinuate my delicate wife
has any resemblance to that double-chinned,

dull as dish-water wench, Dulcinea.
Once you have laughed your fill,
I suggest that you think more deeply
about what kind of impression you will create
when I get around to publishing our correspondence.
People everywhere want to believe that Immortals
are models of good taste and propriety.
Are you going to squander your supernal gifts
and risk your reputation on stupid puns?

O Immortal Ones, let us return respect for respect!
Since I have managed somehow to secure your attention,
I am going to honor your request
for a sample of my work. I tremble at the thought
you may lump me in with those dodo-bird poets,
so, I have done the prudent thing
and chose as a springboard
Li Bai's poem, "Seeing Off Meng Haoran
for Guanling at Yellow Crane Tower."
No fancy twists or flips for me, but already I feel I am
being bounced up towards you—next stop Immortality!

SOS from a Bar of Kiss My Face Soap
(After Li Bai)

My friend, I am headed towards extinction sometime soon.
The Magnolia tree is already in bloom. I am getting

thinner and smaller each time you shower. Please, don't
let me slip through your fingers, pass down the drain.
Stick me onto a fresh bar of soap—that's my only hope!

You will note that I haven't slavishly
imitated the original
but have reversed the perspective
to express the feelings of the departing "friend,"
not the poet who is left behind.
Perhaps, you'll object that the speaker in the poem
is not a human subject but an inanimate object.
I take my cue from animist traditions
from around the world:
if stones can be honored with special powers
why not an object we fondle gratefully every day?

Respectfully yours,

xxxxxxxx xxxxxxx xxxxxx
(aka *Qi Ho-tei*)

An Assignment

Dear *Qi Ho-tei*
(aka Man of La Manchukuo):

We've got to hand it to you—
you beat us to "Russian Auntie."
That's a good one, but don't think
it lets you off the hook.
We know how much you are trying
to suck-up to us
with that pastiche you wrote.

Li Bai himself guffawed and said
maybe you should try a bar
of *Kiss My Ass* soap—
that's how unimpressed he was.
Talk about pathetic fallacy,
just imagine if you had to deal everyday
with all of the inanimate objects surrounding you
voicing their feelings
like a touchy retinue of ungrateful servants.

Do you want to hear the screams of your spoon
plunged into a steaming bowl of soup?
Your fork's unseemly grunts
as you jab its tines into crispy duck?

Or listen to the disdain
when you forget to wipe your greasy lips
as you raise that glass of champagne?
Be thankful the lamentations
of whatever you plop down upon,
be it cushion or commode,
have never been recorded.

The possibilities are endless,
which is why Classical Chinese poets have always been
Mindful of maintaining clear distinctions
between persons, places, and things.
Cheng Ming is the term you need to study as a poet.
Forget *anime* and Disney cartoons.
Your job is to maintain the natural order of the world
by upholding organic categories.
Don't spread delusion.
Know the proper name and function
of whatever can be named.

Jeez, why would you even want to buy
that insipidly named bar of soap?
If you want to know how to title something,
go study the menu from a Chinese restaurant.
You'll leap at the chance to order—

Eagles Open Up Their Wings,

Dragon Hiding In A Jade Palace
Ants Climbing Trees
Buddha Jumps Over The Wall

Even the chefs in China are more poetic
than those *New Yorker* poets!

Ok, it's time for you to get down to basics.
Here's an assignment for you.
Remind yourself what it means to be
at home in your own body.
Get in touch with the "four dignities."
No, they are not the pompous figures
you probably are imagining!
We are referring to
the fundamental modes of action
that make us fully human:
Standing, Lying, Sitting, and *Walking.*
If you haven't mastered them
how will you ever ground your poetry?

Good luck with that—we're hoping to read
another sample of your work.
If you can impress us with your sincerity
and quit trying to be oh, so clever
by hijacking one of our proven poems,
you may win us over in the end.

We'll even consider awarding you with a new name
that doesn't conjure up a lost cause.

I have the honor to speak for the Eight Immortals,

J' Han-shan
Peach Blossom Spring
Somewhere near Wu Ling

P.S. Take a tip from me—this gang of Eight Immortals,
whom I serve day-in, day-out, only got to be Immortal
because they followed the first precept of the Great Learning:

Look straight into the heart
and watch with affection
the way people grow.

That's what Chinese-Chinese poets do! —JHS

"If I Were a Better Confucian"

c/o J' Han-shan
Peach Blossom Spring
Somewhere near Wu Ling

Dear Champions of No Twisty Thoughts:

I don't know what you imagine when you order
"Eagles Open Up Their Wings."
I canot help but picture a soaring carnivore
who lets fall on my plate a rodent-sized carcass
ripped to shreds by its beak.
In the land famous for monkey brain sushi,
that sounds par for the course (no pun intended).
God, the exotic shit you guys eat!
I bet your "Dragon Hiding in a Jade Palace"
is something lizard-y and hot like a chili-stuffed gecko
embedded in a sickly green aspic.
Tell me, what kind of joke is it
that a vegetarian monk would jump over
the wall of his monastery
for a bowl of soup made from the fin
of a man-eating shark?
Even more school-boyish is to name
a dish of minced meat and noodles
"Ants Climbing Trees."

But, hey, you have a point about
the poetic pretensions of your old-time chefs.
Their instinctive adherence to
Symbolism and Dada is more fun than
the begrudging Post-Modernism
of those *New Yorker* poets.

Secondly, O Masters of the Mixed Message
you mock my contemporaries
for not being as transcendent as your beloved Li Bai
whose wine-soaked mind
soared to the heavens where he joined
with you, his fellow drunkards!
Ok—that may be a cultural thing, acceptable
in its own time and place.
But why then do you make such a big deal
about me needing to be grounded
by your so-called dignities?
It's especially galling when I think how
you guys three-sheets-to-the-wind
at one of your debaucheries
can neither stand nor sit in a proper manner,
much less walk in a straight line
before you pass out and hit the deck.
Oh, how dignified you must look to the servants
who hook their arms under your armpits
and lift you into perfumed beds,

so you can sleep off your drunkenness
in some dreamless stupor.

Is it indelicate of me to suggest
you're talking out of both sides of your mouth?
I am beginning to think
you might actually prefer I become
some kind of flightless dodo.
Be that as it may, I am not extinct yet!
Ready or not, here I come with a new poem.
Make of it what you will.

This is Not a Chinese-Chinese Poem

No Springtime peonies in this poem,
no summer cicadas,
not one falling maple leaf.
No cold winter flakes.

It is not midnight under a starry sky,
nor morning tinted with rosy light.

I am neither shooting rapids
through the Three Gorges
nor riding horseback up a mountain
called Incense-Burner Peak.

I am stuck, instead, standing in line
under the fluorescent lights
of my local CVS
waiting with others to pick up
prescriptions,
counted out one pill at a time
from billions upon billions of pills
pushed each year by companies
making so much hay
off those miserable copays
you bet they got
a Mandate from Heaven!

Given all of the side-effects
and addictions,
maybe we would be better off
taking quaint concoctions
of roots and herbs, or even sketchy
immortal-making elixirs
once peddled by Taoist sages.

Something is in the air
that causes everyone here to look
so ill-dressed, decidedly not
at his or her best.
If I were a better Confucian
I would gaze straight into my heart

and watch with affection
the way people grow.

Truth is, I can't wait
to get on home and leave behind
this random sampling
of what happens in time
to the Human Form Divine.

Yours Truly,

XXXXXXXX XXXXXXX XXXXXX

"The Gate-less Gate"

Dear *Bao Wao* :

Yes, that's you, formerly addressed as
Qi Ho-tei and *Rong Wei.*
We will get to the reason we decided to rename you,
but first we need to address your latest diatribe
against Chinese cuisine and the drinking
habits of Immortal poets.
It is surprising to think that someone like you
who has expressed a burning desire to be
a Chinese poet could be so negative
about the bedrock of Chinese culture—its food!
Every native Chinese when served
the elegantly named dish
Eagles Open Up Their Wings
would automatically feel awe-struck
at the mere mention of such a noble bird
preparing for flight, but far from
internalizing the exhilarating rush of
wind ruffling feathers, you focus
on the most gruesome detail you can think of.
The same cynical propensity keeps recurring in your
interpretation of each item on the menu.
Suffice it to say you have no idea that poetic language

should speak to our better angels,
not to mention, set the stage for delightful gustation.

Indeed, you could be a better Confucian
and a better Taoist too.
Unlike Robert Bly, the leaps you take in your mind
are usually in the wrong direction.
Go ahead, be a literalist and worry about
the salmonella and parasites
lurking in that skewered gecko seared
on an open flame.
Li Bai casting his eye on the same dish
would be transported up to the Heavens on the back
of a smoke-trailing magical beast
while you are still thinking barbecue!
Really, you seem to have no clue
what goes on inside a Divine Lover's Mind.
Don't be fooled by appearances.
What's the difference between one of our Immortals
"passed out" on the floor and
Socrates standing transfixed
in a doorway for hours on end?
Who is to say whether he has lost his mind
or is contemplating Love itself?
One thing for sure we would feel right at home
with him at one of those Symposia
where he drank everyone under the table.

No mortal Greek would outdo us in
pouring-out libations
to the God of Wine! And oh, the panegyrics
we could deliver on whatever topic
might catch the fancy of those overprivileged *poofters*,
while you sit there in the corner of the room
like a Presbyterian
looking pinch-faced and sober.

In your last letter, you also took us to task
for "talking out of both sides of our mouth at once."
We had to look-up that expression in a textbook
of *Communicative English.*
(Gee, is there any other kind?)
What an interesting idiom—we were surprised to learn
that it is taken as a negative thing in your world.
It seemed to us if you could utter speech
out of the left side and right side of your
mouth at the same time
that would be considered a remarkable talent.
People in our day would have paid handsomely
to see such a ventriloquist, but, no,
our book says it refers to
someone like a politician who continually changes
his position and ends up sounding
"duplicitous and untrustworthy."

It is painful to think you were accusing us
of not upholding *cheng ming,*
the very same principle we had brought
to your attention in our last letter.

One of our cooler heads suggested
we shouldn't take your insult so seriously—
that you were just being defensive
because we were too harsh in our criticism
of your penchant for pathetic fallacy.

Perhaps, you were also offended that we suggested
you needed to get down to basics
before you can compete with an Immortal poet
like Li Bai. Those four dignities, by the way,
are not relegated to your physical posture alone.
Need we remind you of Ezra Pound's gloss on the
character, *hsin*—

信

His reading of its two elements
gives him a metaphor that works as well
in English as in Chinese—
"A man standing by (his) word."
This is one of the rare instances in which a character

can actually be seen as a pictograph.
How is this for speaking out of both
sides of your mouth!
On the left is "man" and on the right "word."
Together they mean "sincerity,"
a virtue most definitely honored by us
and, we trust, in your better moments by you, too!
Pay close attention, here—
not only must you stand by your words,
you've got to sit with them, lie down with them,
and take your daily walk with them.
In short, as Flaubert would say, finding the *mot*
that is *juste* is the ultimate test
of a writer's honesty,
requiring non-stop attention.

Are you getting sick of our advice?
After all, when you first contacted us,
you weren't asking how to become
a better poet or even a poet at all!
You simply wanted our stamp of approval
on what you thought was a done deal.
To paraphrase an old Ch'an saying, such a request
raises waves where there is no wind,
gouges a wound in healthy flesh···
asks for a stick to hit the moon.

How impossible that sounds!
But take heart—the gate you are seeking
a way through, around, or over
is a "gate-less gate."
It may at first seem impenetrable as a wall,
but "gate-less" means there is Nothing
in front of you to open
and Nothing behind you to close.
It's just a big fat Nothing for you to confront
like the generations of meditating-sitters before you
who have swallowed *"Wu"*
Chao-chou's answer to the question,

"Has a dog Buddha-nature or not?"

This is not a koan for *Rong Wei* or *Qi Ho-tei.*
Only you *Bao Wao* with your new name
can rise to the occasion and explain
what *Chao-chou* meant by his resounding

"Not."

Take up the challenge little brother—
gnaw on your bone, suck out the marrow,
show others the Way!

As always, I have the honor to speak for
the Eight Immortals,

J'Han-shan
Peach Blossom Spring
Somewhere near Wu Ling

P.S. The Immortals wanted me to add that they are all pulling for
your land to improve its medical system. Single-payer or not, you
have got to bring down those drug prices! We know a thing or two
about the evil manipulation of harmful substances. Think of the
imperialistic shenanigans that caused the Opium Wars. —JHS

III

A Sampling of Poems from
The Pavilion for Washing Away Thoughts

He said: the wise delight in water,
the humane delight in hills.
The knowing are active, the humane tranquil.

— Analects, Bk VI, Ch. XXI

The Swing

for my brother on his
80th birthday

1.

In the space of your imagination
where the moon comes and goes on a spring night,
the kind Chinese poets would pay
a 1,000 gold coins
             for just one hour,

breathe deep and take in
the clear scent of flowers threaded with
sounds of flutes and songs
coming from an upstairs window
overlooking tree tops and a stepping-stone path
wending to the point
where the garden
             holds most still.

There—you'll find a swing
suspended from chains in a wooden frame.
The seat always appears empty,
always waiting for someone to sit down
and rock back and forth.

Su Tung-p'o saw his own emptiness
in this swing and tossed off
a few lines that would maintain
the equilibrium of a scene that exists
for us unchanged, no matter
how long ago the un-named revelers
scattered like blossoms, the garden grew
into a tangle, and the whole tradition
of civil servants examined
on poetry
                    came to an end.

2.

Su Tung-p'o went on to write
many poems—he led a complicated life,
pitting himself against authority,
inevitably suffering exile,
even imprisonment for displeasing
the Emperor in some of those poems.
And here I am prattling on,
never having rankled an exalted ruler
nor come up with a signature image
that would stick
                    in your mind.

No red wheelbarrow for me,
no petals on a wet, black bough!

I thought the best I could do in a poem
honoring your inner self
was to draw attention to Su Tung-p'o's
swing, poised at the heart
of a garden on a deep, still night.

Then I remembered how every day
you can look out your window
over the whole Pacific Ocean
stretching from the Sayulita coast
to the horizon and beyond to China—
a nightmare for an agoraphobe,
a boon, though, for a long-time
devotee of The Great Mother.
You hardly need my exhortation
to embrace the immensity
of Her bosom to your bosom.
You have chosen your site well.

3.

Now my poem moves between
two poles —dappled night

and dazzling day, what's intimate
and far away. Your character

seated in its heart's swing is
hung on matrilineal traits—
self-effacement, aesthetic gift,
rumination, punning wit.

Laughing off your fate when
the table-saw took your middle
fingers, you were the first
to make the "call me" gesture!

But lacking a steady signal
from limbs to brain, it's harder
to stay upright on your feet.
Take a pill not to wobble

or clear the fog? Adapt, adapt
is the key to aging: give up
that two-wheeled bike for
a recumbent fixed to the floor;

don't stray too far from a Men's
Room door; and never forget
uprightness like stature is
not only physical but moral.

If there's a perk in slowing
down, it's how your goodness
seems to grow. Once you
were the epitome of cool, now

your essential kindness rules.
I can see the love you've
earned in your children's and
grandchild's eyes, and

note the tenderness shown
by your three remarkable
wives willing for a weekend
to re-unite their former

families into one big Family.
Tonight, in this hall we'll
toast enduring ties. We may
not have jade cups to raise

or "vermilioned" dancers in
transparent brocade, but
who's to say our celebration
is less deserving of a poem

than Su Tung-p'o's reverie?
Have faith—each hour spent

together is worth a 1,000
gold coins (no poet has seen!)

"The Joy of Fishes"

Water spills over limestone rocks
in the falls below the *Garden of Flowing Fragrance*
and runs down the slope past
the Pavilion for Washing Away Thoughts.

The rocks themselves once submerged
in Lake Tai are the real thing
imported at great expense to complement
the garden's Suzhou-style pond.

A plaque encourages visitors to imagine
long-deceased literati delighting
in water, feeling amity with hills and peaks,
jagged ones wreathed in mist.

If you look beyond the pavilion's thatched,
roof, over the tops of California oak,
you'll see a range of cloudless mountains
covered in chaparral, not bamboo.

Sunlight angles into the pavilion where I sit
as the garden's accidental recluse,
my two ears the only two ears at the moment
washed by the sound of the falls.

In front of me, images of branches and leaves
are rippled in the gentle stream.
Fish no bigger than slivers are suspended
in the water beneath, only inches deep.

When they dart, they move like thought itself
in directions you cannot predict.
They scatter so fast! Then before you know it,
the fish reappear in different spots.

Never thirsty—always clean—what need
have they to purify their Mind?
"I know the joy they take in their element
from the joy I take in mine."

Writing on Walls

What to make of those famous poets
who traveled around China
and would have us believe they left poems
on monastery walls?
Guest books I can understand,
but walls? They never say
if they had been invited or given permission
to post a poem on the spot
for either the Buddha or posterity's sake.
Consider Su Tung-p'o—is it really possible
he took it upon himself
to inscribe characters on Abbot Lun's
plaster wall, even after
the closed-lip master had met
his queries about The Way in perfect silence?

Did he have the chutzpah to leap up in front
of the sangha or did he wait until
the room had emptied out, and he could
sneak back in and work unseen?
Maybe, the whole monastery-wall-thing
is just a trope and later poets
following the golden age of the Tang
composed the poems in the privacy
of their studies at home, sparing themselves

the bother to commit them to memory
before they journeyed back
down the mountain and sent them off
to the printers, so they could be enjoyed
by an audience more receptive
than the ill-fed, disinterested monks.

As for the poem Su Tung-p'o bequeathed
the monastery and now us,
what kind of provocation was it
to volunteer to the enlightened Abbot
a teaching tale about a man who
tossed and turned all night because
he couldn't recall if his beard
habitually rested on top of his covers
or was tucked beneath? So vexing
was this shaggy-dog koan when morning
finally came the poor old-guy
wanted to yank-out his whiskers
by their roots! Only the Abbot knows
for sure if this story is as silly
as it sounds or has "deep meaning."

Kudos, in any case, to Su Tung-p'o.
Classical lyrics appear so casual
in free-verse translation, but
Chinese readers know what it takes

to wing those intricate patterns
of tones and rhymes and fit them
into place line after line.
Imagine him standing with the tip
of his brush poised to make
the first downward stroke,
a thousand years of Tradition
coursing through his mind
as the Empty wall threatens
to swallow him up. In that split
second, you can hear him think—

"If I'm to get the Abbot to crack a smile,
first thought better be best thought."

Hands-on, Hands-off

A few well-placed stones   can turn water run-off
into a slalom   easier on the slope
than a straight downhill course   that leaves in its path
a gully, a gash   as top-soil is carried away fast.

Cover, even stubble   breaks the force of rain drops,
protects roots beneath trees   swales, too, help you
harvest water   not waste it.

When hiking in the high country   over boulder
and scree   find a smooth pebble   put it on
your tongue   suck on it   you'll feel less thirsty.

In Holland   twisting your torso
as you open the car door   with the hand furthest
from the handle   saves a cyclist
speeding past   from a stupid crash.

Okinawans getting up from   and sitting down
on tatami mat-floors   practice everyday-yoga
live longer   more limber lives.

Hands-on medicine can avert   disabling disease
the master who turns back   an attack

with his fingertips alone   knows how to channel *chi*
he can step aside   roll with the punches

or bend like bamboo   in a breeze.

Mountain Lion Country

"Mountain lion country," the sign says
put up a day ago in our own Arroyo Seco
where pedigreed dogs of all breeds
are devotedly walked by their owners on cells,
bagging poop, talking the talk.
More than half of California, including LA,
is the natural habitat of long-tailed carnivorous cats,
which means there must be deer somewhere near,
though in sixty odd years,
I've yet to see evidence of them or the lions living here.
Stressed by fire and drought,
on the prowl for their phantom quarry,
are the big cats making forays down from the mountains
past the all-night lights of JPL
and the cheering ghost crowds
of an emptied Rose Bowl?
Must lords in the food chain, haunted
by the sound of hooves clattering over rocks,
across asphalt, scrounge like coyotes
for the Arroyo's daily potluck
of ground squirrel, rabbit, and raccoon?
O to hunker down over a real meal!
It takes only two bipeds (minus twitchy white tails)
to equal one bounding deer.

Even the uncouth, history tells us,
can get used to flesh
less gamey, more tender to the tooth.

The park rangers who worry for our safety
say, "don't walk, jog, or bike alone,"
especially at dawn and dusk.
After you leave your car and follow
the channeled creek in earshot of its trickling runoff,
be on the lookout for a soundless,
solo predator slipping through live oak
and eucalyptus shadows, the bird-flitted brush.
Out in the open, it disappears like Waldo
into its camouflaging coat,
the same color as the sun-burnt hillside ahead,
the sandy trail underfoot. Inscrutable feline—
known for unpredictable and sudden attacks,
per chance it singles you out,
don't turn your back or try to shrink from sight
even if your body is messaging "instant flight."
Stand tall, lift a child onto your shoulders
and make yourself taller, wave arms wildly and shout.
"If that fails, throw stones." That's right stones!
which you've got to hunt around for,
stoop down, grab from the pebble-strewn path,
then aim and fling—once, twice, thrice—
before your lion already locked-on

like a heat-seeking device, comes close enough
on padded feet to spring into the air—
claws open, teeth bared—heading straight for
your panic-stricken throat in one swift
and unbelievably fluid leap—horrific as that!

Another alternative (strictly off record)
is to drop your pet's leash like
one of Hippomenes' golden apples.
And hope the lion is diverted
as easily as greedy Atalanta, while you
back-pedal back to the parking lot
and return home alone, bereft and chastened.
The next time you walk the Arroyo,
if feeling jumpy, forego sacrifice and stones
and bring a spray-can of Counter-Assault.
Cats, like grizzlies, hate being stung in the eyes.
When a stealth attack is launched,
the trick is in timing the pepper-cloud's release
into the stalker's oncoming face—
too soon is as risky as too late.
That said—listen up suburban America!
Put to test in a narrow corridor of wilderness,
neither God nor beast shall forgive us our trespass.
Only we can do the civilized thing
and forgive them just enough
who now and again trespass against us.

Sooner or later, we'll learn
it's less harmful all around to be more Taoist
than Monopolist—to find ways
to accommodate fellow interlopers,
not blow them away.
Some Founder must have said it—

"The country works best for every one of us
when in *non-action* we trust."

You Can't Make a Mirror
by Polishing a Tile

I am just an ordinary guy living
an ordinary life,
attracted to the idea that Ordinary Mind
is Buddha Mind, too.
If I had been raised by a Tiger Mom,
I wouldn't have a Chinaman's
chance to be ordinary—
Buddha Mind and Extraordinary Mind
would be one and the same
and meant to be mine.
Lucky for me, I can't get a new Mom—
being perfectly ordinary
will always be the name of my game.

Eager to know if I could go about
my ordinary business and have it All,
I googled Ordinary Mind.
And found out that Mazu Dao-yi
way back in the Tang
first said, "Ordinary Mind is the Way."
So far, so good, but take note—
Mazu himself was every bit extraordinary:
"He strode like a bull,

glared like a tiger,
and had trained his tongue
to touch his nose."
That alone is a tip-off
that his Ordinary Mind might not be so ordinary,
in fact, it may not even be a mind!
At least, in the way we think of minds.

Try to imagine your mind
making no judgements,
holding no "likes,"
initiating no goal-oriented actions,
and eschewing all dualistic thoughts.
You would see nothing
as profane, nothing as sacred.
Birth and Death, Time and Eternity
would cease to exist
along with every little vanity
that keeps your ego afloat.
Talk about narrowing the field!
A mind too fine to use
is not the mind
of an ordinary guy trying to get by.
Nor even that of a Bodhisattva
who sacrifices Nirvana
for the sake of all mankind.

Credulous me—to believe
that when I plop myself down
on an outdoor chair
in earshot of the freeway
and the neighbors' blowers,
I'm not just putting off
sweeping leaves, pulling weeds,
but exercising Buddha Mind
like a Master aligning his chi
with the Empty chimes
hung under his temple's eaves.
You can bet old Mazu
wouldn't trade his fearsome mind
for my lax mind,
much less claim my "practice"
embodied the Way.
If never our two minds shall meet,
just exactly how nondual
is his Nondualism?
Why does he keep Ordinary Mind
from being truly ordinary?
How did that proviso of non-defilement
sneak into his teaching
when strictly speaking
the Nothing that is there
can never be defiled?

Logic is not my strength,
but I will try to reason this out.
Mind itself is Buddha.
Buddha means "awakened."
An individual mind, both yours and mine,
are One with Mind.
Therefore, our minds are both awakened,
which sounds great,
except I must confess I have no sense
of having been awakened.
Tell me, what's the meaning of that?
Shall I get excited
by a default state of Mind
that's always the same
for everyone, everywhere
no matter what we think or do?
It all seems so definitional
like "Duh, isn't the sky blue?"

Now I am really in the weeds.
I should keep my ordinary mouth shut—
let Buddha Mind and Ordinary Mind
take a well-earned rest.
One last thing, though, about spiritual practice—
Mazu's teacher said,
"polish a tile everyday,

you won't make a beautiful mirror."
I say no problem:

What you get is a beautiful tile.

New Year's Letter to
The Improbably Elected Leader of
The Less than Free World

Like the Emperor of China
who plowed a furrow once a year
to illustrate "the strength of men is in grain,"
you too can make a grand gesture—

run a mower over a putting green,
tuck in sheets in one of your garish suites,
grill a rare Rump [sic] steak, prepare
a taco bowl, wearing your fat red tie.

No one is better at fulfilling
"the poor man's idea of a rich man's success."
You are truly a modern Midas!
You turn shit to gold and gold to shit.

Too late now for a course correction,
shit has already hit the fan. When
all is said and done, History will send you
up shit-creek without a paddle.

And make you eat a shit-sandwich too!

Never yours,

xxxxxxxx xxxxxxx xxxxxx

News from Jiangxi Province

Fifty-eight years after the flooded Hongmen Gorges
filled up with water,
                  and the new reservoir

mapped itself like a dragon
perpetually rampant on snaky limbs
crackling with blue fire,

a Ming Dynasty Buddha, carved on the cliff-face
above the confluence at Xiaoshi, centuries
before the ancient town was drowned,
pokes its forgotten head above the placid surface
of the man-made lake,
                  the water-level having

dropped to its shoulders while engineers renovate
the reservoir's hydropower gates.

Its gaze is still directed downward and inward
as though receiving prayers from anxious boatmen
poling through crosscurrents and choppy waves,
the same medium that sank
                    sixty-three towns

and whatever was part of their bustling lives

that couldn't be carried away.

Blacksmith Huang Keping, 82, remembers
the curling incense in the small temple
at the foot of the statue that had been gilded
in gold, the thin foil
                    long since floated off

in little flecks from the chiseled stone.

Being submerged below now seems
less like a banishment, more a safe haven
from gritty winds
                    and the unpitying blows

of Red Guard hammers
crushing one of the "Four Olds."

When spring rains arrive in March,
the knobby head will sink once again from
sight, only to be seen by the divers
whose duty is to research and protect
the State's underwater relics.

How tables turn!

After Bamiyan, we've all been hoping for

redemptive signs. Dynasties come
and go—no telling when Buddhas will
appear and disappear.

In this distant province, where for better
and worse men have harnessed
the Spirit of the Valley, take note—
what pools as easily as it flows
is older than
                    the oldest of "Olds,"

common to all and close to the Way itself.

Call it Yin if you like, but is there
anything Dark and Mysterious
in an element without color and scent?
Watch it slip through
                    your fingers,
sluice off your body—
hide itself behind clear glass.

If not stirred, muddied, or made turbid,
Light can shine through it
down to remarkable depths.

Think of the 10,000 Things drinking it in!

No License

It has come down to this: you are asked to believe
that your spiritual teacher, who just slugged a nun
in her belly, is an enlightened master, schooled
in Crazy Wisdom, in effect, a Buddha himself.
How is it the Realized get to leap-frog over those
Ten Grave Precepts the rest of us are exhorted
to uphold? The relevant one in this case being—
"Not indulging in anger." Transcending duality
is not like having your cake and eating it too.
One suspects satori is only momentary at best,
hard to get, even harder to hold. It's not a license
for licentiousness, a divine pass for anything goes.

This much I've gleaned—demand that teachers,
either incarnated or self-made, square the things
they say with the things they do. Subject as we
all are to the moving lines of Yin and Yang don't
apologize for being hung-up on the difference
between Weak and Strong, Light and Dark,
Right and Wrong. For Mencius, benevolence
sprouts naturally—who wouldn't reach out
to save a child teetering on the edge of a well?
Punching Lama says, "the harder I hit the deeper
the connection." Trust yourself if it hurts like hell.
At the very least, insist that kindness be upheld.

"Monkey and Crab"

One hand at the end of his outstretched arm
grasps the tapered top
                    of a bamboo stalk,

bent down by the full weight of his
fuzzy-white body
dropped like a plumb-bob beneath.

The other arm
fully extended to the tips of sumi-black fingers
strains to grab
                    a delicate crab,

pincers up scuttling across the ground.

Except there is no ground—
only the space where the ground would be,
above which is projected the monkey

and a cluster of
spiky black leaves.

*

"Monkey and Crab" used to hang in the dining room
above the mantelpiece behind my mother's seat
facing my father.
                    Now it's hung
in the bedroom
opposite the mirrored-wall left of the bed
where my wife and I sleep.

The monkey reminds us of our Mind,
and the crab just of reach is whatever we desire.

Such a happy monkey!
He still thinks he'll get some sweet meat yet,
that the sweetest part is in the claws.

Embracing Empty Mountains, Cold Creeks

How cool was it at nineteen reading
Gary Snyder's translations of Han-shan's
Cold Mountain poems in West Coast
Beat-Speak as though the Chinese hermit
were a fellow lookout, looking down
from a station on Sourdough Peak—

"They don't get what I say
& I don't talk their language.
All I can say to those I meet:
'Try and make it to Cold Mountain.'"

I didn't take the challenge literally,
but the idealized figure of a drop-out
monk who inscribed hipper
than hip poems on rocks and cliffs
entered my pantheon and went
unquestioned for fifty years,
until a few days ago when I opened
a translation of Meng Chiao's
later poems and read these lines—

Invariably pure and austere, poets mostly
starve to death embracing empty mountains.

It's not like Cold Mountain itself
came tumbling down, but I felt some
kind of tectonic shift as I read
how the Shang poets Po Yi and Shu Ch'i
took to the wilderness
and died from cold and hunger.
Too politically correct to eat
the grain of the conquering Chou!

Their empty mountains,
many dynasties before the spread
of Taoism and Ch'an, meant
empty bellies, not Empty Mind.
If they couldn't fill themselves up
with ferns, how is it Han Shan
could survive his winters, as he boasts,
by "building a little fire⋯
boiling some greens"?

Meng Chiao's "mostly" suggests
he would cast a cold eye
on such a claim. I bet he'd
be skeptical, too, of Snyder's
romantic notion you can
sometimes run into Immortals like
Han-shan in "the skid rows,

orchards, hobo jungles,
and logging camps of America."

Who knows, maybe, there was
a Golden Age for displaced
males from the thirties up through
the sixties? Thinking, though,
of the millions of strung-out men
and women on the streets today,
you might well ask how many
homeless does it take across
centuries (and oceans, mind you)
to create just one Han-shan?

If I were still teaching poetry,
I would caution my students.
There's no real proof of Han-shan's
existence beyond an apocryphal biography
and the iconic prints of himself
laughing with his side-kick Shih-te.
According to legend,
whenever they met, they clapped
their hands and shouted out
their "Ha! Ha!" mantra.
No need for them to recite
hard-to-pronounce sutras.

On Cold Mountain, we're told,
"The spirit is enlightened of itself."

Han-shan like Homer
may have been a single poet
or an entire school of poets.
That in itself is not an issue for me
as long as the poems speak
for themselves which they do
because their style
is colloquial and fresh.
You can read them as Buddhist,
Taoist, or Ch'an. They don't
belong to any one sect.

Was the Han-shan I imagine
the exception to Meng Chiao's
rule, not so *pure nor austere?*
Good for him! if somehow
his mountain-madman practice
kept him alive. I can't help
but cheer the rag-tag persona—
his birch-bark hat, wooden shoes,
the unruly hair, how he yelled
"Thief, thief" at the servant sent
to his cave to give him a set
of new clothes. It only sounds

"crazy" at first. Ruminate
a bit and it turns into a koan.
Nothing crazy, either, picking
a site that is hiking distance
to a temple-kitchen, no further,
I suspect, then the saunter
from Walden Pond to Concord.

What touches me now is
the intensity of Meng Chiao's
heart-songs more in tune
with the howling and snarling
in the everyday frenzies
of wind and water gnawing
deep gorges than the stillness
of an empty mountainside.
Placing himself at the bottom
of the precipitous chasms,
he laments the suffering of
his fellow creatures—*chants
for their thousand worries
renewed*—and never exalts in
having risen above them,
sitting high-up in white clouds.

Ironically, the Cold Creek
where he sips wine at dawn

feels even colder than Han Shan's
retreat and just as wild.
Frozen into blades, the rapids
slice open ducks, rip apart geese,
and clatter loud as white jade
against the hulls of boats
made famous for carrying
on board exiled poets heading
downstream towards
some miserable posting
far from friends
and a longed-for homeland.

In dead of winter, we must have faith
that the Way flowing past shores
like a priceless mirror
ablaze with heaven's light
will put away its swords,
unsheathe the warm air,
and lift us up with fragrant scents.

This is the exam question I would set
for my students—mostly, myself:

"When the great ideals of your life seem
to have run their course, where
do you find the courage not to stay stuck,

113

to make it new day by day?"

Here's a clue from the shabby robed
Meng Chiao who still strove
in old age to turn his "words···into
stately peaks and summits":

Windblown,

        last ice shudders on the creek···

Blossoms

      drip

        and drip

          and drip....

Suddenly,

      as if all sword wounds were over,

the body of a hundred battles
begins rising.

Thanksgiving Time

> "Do not assist to grow."
> —Bk. II, *Mencius*

Now's the time we practice
being thankful for what has passed.

If the flowering chamiso once bright yellow
looks dingy as a dog's uncombed coat,
just wait—when the sun catches
the silky filaments at each twig's end,
the bushes will turn

                    champagne gold!
That's the difference
between chamiso and retirees
who work so hard

not to go to seed, become old.

Commentary

A few days ago on my birthday, the same day that the Foreword to this intriguing collection of letters and poems was dated, my quizzical, name-phobic friend yyyyyyy yyyyyy yyyyy asked me directly if I would like to provide some textual commentary. It was a gesture on his part of pure friendship. He knows how important it is for retirees to feel useful. What the hell, I am flattered he thinks I can handle the job. At the same time, I am also feeling apprehensive—rusty, actually. I can't even remember the last time I wrote an academic essay. I hope I can shift into high gear and find something worthwhile to say. The pressure must be getting to me. Now, all I can hear in my head is my former guru quoting the poet-saint Nipat Niranjan— "If you pluck a pubic hair off a corpse, will you make it any lighter?" The opposite, I trust, also holds true—one more pubic hair added to a corpse will not make it any heavier.

Okay, no need to chase that rabbit! Let me keep my eye on the ball. Right off the bat, we must ask— "Just exactly where can we find these translations that have set the scholarly world astir?" My immediate google search did not turn up any sites. As far as I can tell, no online journal or blog has posted any poems in English by *Bao Wao*. When I typed in his name, the algorithm-machine gave me Wow Bao, a Chicago restaurant-chain that advertises "hot Asian buns." No, it's not a Chinese Hooters, but at this rate don't be surprised if "The Eight Immortals" turns out to be a 50's doo-wop group from neighboring Mo Town. The striking absence of *Bao Wao*'s name, in any case, is highly problematic. What are we to think, if no one besides yyyyyyyy yyyyyyy yyyyyy has ever read or heard of him before the publication of this book? You can imagine how embarrassed I feel having to declare at the outset that my friend seems to be fibbing. Perhaps, it doesn't matter if a poet going by the name of *Bao Wao* has never appeared online or in print. What's most important is that yyyyyyyy yyyyyyy yyyyyy is deeply committed to these so-called "translations" however they came into his hands. I can assure you that his literary judgement is impeccable even if he is guilty of overselling his poet, whose true identity has yet to be spelled out.

No question "The Joy of Fishes" is a fine poem, and the *Garden of Flowing Fragrance* is a fine garden (even if the plants don't seem especially fragrant.) I have been there many times, and like my friend I prefer to go on Tuesdays when it is closed to the general public. It is also the day the watering-lady makes her rounds. I enjoy chatting with her while she keeps an eye on her wristwatch to make sure that she doesn't under or over-water her succulents. She is quite friendly, but how ridiculous of yyyyyyyy yyyyyyy yyyyyy to leap to the conclusion that she had been talking to a Chinese poet with the first-

117

name *Wao.* A woman old enough to remember when her daily intake of CBD came in nickel bags was obviously saying, "Oh, **wow** ····." My friend yyyyyyyy yyyyyyy yyyyyy may have ears like a hunting dog (not to mention ESP), but—God bless him—he doesn't always understand what he "hears" through whatever faculty he employs. Truth is there is no proof that the watering-lady was addressing *Bao Wao.* Her casual exclamation that she is looking forward to reading "those poems" tells us nothing about who wrote them. I am afraid my life is too short to interview every elderly, bearded academic with wire-rim glasses who frequents the library! We hope, in any case, that she will get to read the poems when this book goes on sale at the Huntington Library's gift shop.

The vision of yyyyyyyy yyyyyyy yyyyyy running around the garden seeking the elusive *Bao Wao* is quite amusing. It is entirely in keeping with his scholarly compulsions that he would hurry home and start reading Kusan's fable again. I beg to differ, though, about the identity of "The Source." The original text does not call it "Peach Blossom Spring." True, the line accompanying the illustration says the blossoms falling in the "emerald water" are "red," but peach blossoms are not uniformly red like petals on flowering quince, crepe myrtle, or exotic *flame-of-the-forest* trees. Click on Google Images —you'll see peach blossoms are pink except for the blushing red centers inside the flower's cup. My friend's habitual skewing of the truth should give us pause. Remember, he is the one who is responsible for that internal downloading of the letters and poems that make up this book. Oh boy, where to start?

First of all, we shouldn't assume that he even knows which group of Eight Immortals he has contacted. One is transcendent, the other (in spite of their name) merely mortal. If you look-up the Eight Immortals, Wikipedia will tell you that these Tang Dynasty figures are beloved by Taoists for their ability "to bestow life and destroy evil." All of them, it seems, are well-versed in magical practices and can back up their occult powers by exercising the more down-to-earth, martial art of Qigong, which they apparently invented. Because of their exploits, they have earned the right to live as Immortals in the gold and silver palaces on a group of five islands in the Bohai sea. Their base is Mt. Penglai, known for its absence of cold weather and suffering. What a place! Magical fruits grow on trees; rice bowls automatically fill themselves, and wine cups are never empty. However ideal it may be, you will note that is far away from "Peach Blossom Spring," which is on the mainland somewhere near Wu Ling. More importantly, these legendary heroes are not poets like "The Eight Immortals of the Wine Cup," the flesh and blood scholars who flocked around the great poet Li Bai and became famous for their drinking. History will tell you they died for normal human reasons, like old age and cirrhosis of the liver. Only their most credulous admirers believe they are living as Immortals on a timeless island or in some utopian world untouched by life as we know it. Whatever is left of their physical remains has been reduced to a mixture of ashes and bones, safely tucked away in memorials and graves, which means actual Immortality for them depends entirely upon cultural memory—i.e. the readers who keep their poetry alive from one generation to the next. Of course, it would still be possible to get in touch with them vicariously by getting blotto and experiencing the momentary transcendence they were so fond of. Another method of contact, if you are not skeptical of paranormal experience, would be to turn inward and communicate directly with their spokesman *J'Han-shan*, just like my friend claims he did.

Speaking of *J'Han-shan*, we need to ask, "Who is he, really?" Sure, we have all heard of the Cold Mountain poet Han-shan, but a near miss in the spelling of his name is as good as a mile, and besides it is more probable that a city sophisticate—not a hermit—would be the spokesperson for those eight literati who first came together in the bustling taverns of Chang'an. This *J'Han-shan's* identity is a true mystery, but utterly crucial since, according to my friend's account, he is the one who is mediating all of the Immortals' responses in the original correspondence with xxxxxxxx xxxxxxx xxxxxx. It is well-worth noting his mailing address is "Peach Blossom Spring," the very same location that was imagined by my friend when he was seeking "the Source." Of course, we know it is not the drinking haunt of those eight famous poets of the Wine Cup, so what gives? Time and space in the world of spirits is far more fluid than ours, hence, there is no reason *J'Han-shan* need exist cheek by jowl with the Immortals in order to channel their sentiments. He could live in "Peach Blossom Spring" or just as easily in the *Garden of Flowing Fragrance*, which is salubrious enough to be compared to Tao Yuanming's utopian paradise. Who knows, maybe *J'Han-shan's* spirit-body, for some karmic reason, inadvertently hitched a ride across the Pacific on one of those fabulously sculpted rocks shipped over from Lake Tai, which xxxxxxxx xxxxxxx xxxxxx calls attention to in "The Joy of Fishes." That's a pretty thought but consider this curious fact—there are eight letters in *J'Han-shan*, the same number as the first set of x's and y's in his two correspondents' inscrutable names (echoing, it would seem, the eight in each group of Immortals.) As a former reader of psychoanalytical criticism, I am compelled to suggest *J'Han-shan* is a subconscious projection of either my friend or xxxxxxxx xxxxxxx xxxxxx.

Far be it from me, though, to insist on Freudian terminology that would demystify the very core of this gathering of letters and poems. I need to respect my friend's cast of mind and life-experience. After all, he grew up in the "Golden Land" of Southern California where esoteric spiritual practice has always been in vogue. The atmosphere is thick with ancient and foreign entities contacted by channelers (and marketers) who claim to be in tune with all sorts of transcendent realms. Why, just a few blocks away in my own Arroyo Seco neighborhood, the rocket-man Jack Parsons and founder of Scientology L. Ron Hubbard infamously engaged in occult sexual rituals in a former craftsman's mansion on Orange Grove Blvd, misnamed—for sure—the *Agape Lodge!* I am relieved to say there is nothing lubricious about *J'Han-shan* nor the Immortals whom he serves. I am not claiming they are perfect models of Confucian rectitude—they are poets, after all, with their reputation for drunkenness to uphold. To his credit, *J'Han-shan* doesn't seem to have any kind of personal agenda. He is humble enough not to make a big deal out of his position. The one instance in the correspondence when he steps out of his role as the Immortals' amanuensis and offers an opinion is neither self-serving nor indiscreet. I can only hope for every reader's sake he is the reliable spokesperson for this Chinese "Dead Poets Society" that he appears to be. As it is, entering into the story that began with my friend's search for *Bao Wao* is like stepping into an Escher print. Believe me, I am still chewing on his admission that he literally turned dizzy at the realization he might have stumbled upon his very own doppelgänger. More and more, this whole project, singularly absent of any evil intent, mind you, is proving to be a benign funhouse of mirrors. It is just like my friend to be involved in some kind of psychic (not physical) five-way with *J'Han-shan*, xxxxxxxx xxxxxxx xxxxxx, Zhang Longxi, and—without my consent—maybe, me too.

That said, I am loathe to contradict the yyyyyyy yyyyyy yyyyyy I have known as a single whole person my entire life. Whatever slip-ups may be spotted in his account, who am I to throw cold water on my friend's claim that the epistolary relationship with the Eight Immortals is a great accomplishment, one that has no precedent in the history of literature? I am certain the letters he transcribed from his inner-mind may strain the credulity of some readers, much as Georgie Hyde-Lees' "automatic" communications challenged Yeats' more rational admirers. One can appreciate what a smart move it was on her part to catch the attention of her newly married husband, who was still mooning over the fifty-one-year-old Maude "Gone" and (who would have thought!) her twenty-three-year-old daughter Iseult. Personally, I don't believe the book that came out of Georgie's subconscious merits all the attention it gets. The outlandish subtitle— "An Explanation of Life Founded upon the Writings of Giraldus and upon Certain Doctrines Attributed to Kusta Ben Luka"—should warn you from taking *A Vision* too seriously. W.H.Auden, for one, was embarrassed by Yeats' occult interests, which he snobbishly labeled as "lower middle-class."

No, worse than that he actually derided his dabbling in mediums, spells, and the Mysterious Orient etc., as being "Southern Californian."[1] I confess that hurts, but I shall take his cultural prejudice in stride. If the naturally gifted Yeats could have distilled such great poetry from "nonsense," then why not give the benefit of the doubt to xxxxxxxx xxxxxxx xxxxxx? No matter how fishy the twelve poems in Part Three may seem as "translations," you can't deny they are accomplished enough to stand on their own as poems, pure and simple.

Ah, but there is nothing *textual* these days that is pure and simple. You can take it to the bank that my former colleagues who came of intellectual age during the rise of Orientalist criticism would get hung-up on the self-serving nature of xxxxxxxx xxxxxxx xxxxxx's idiosyncratic proposal. Wouldn't that be grist for their mill! I can hear them now bristling at the sheer effrontery of an unknown, privileged white male believing he can ignore the living reality of billions of people on the other side of the world. They have got a point. I am half-inclined myself to ask what gives him the right to connect directly with an idealized past that has been and will be forever "exotic" in the minds of his potential readers. To add insult to injury, all of this appropriation by xxxxxxxx xxxxxxx xxxxxx happens effortlessly—he doesn't even have to forgo his own native language! Talk about cultural imperialism, how could we not conclude that this is the latest twist in a long history of Western hegemony? Of course, as long as we are all drinking out of the same proverbial glass, which is either half-full or half-empty, any argument can be turned on its head. Maybe, in time critics will come to view *Correspondence with The Immortals* as a testament to the diversity of a three-thousand-year-old tradition that can welcome an asylum seeker and make him its own. Who is to say China's *hot pot* is not a melting pot? Give it a stir and you'll find the half-Turk, half-Han Li Bai. Why not xxxxxxxx xxxxxx xxxxxx too? Stranger non-native speakers have travelled the Middle Kingdom's old Silk Road. Maybe, the ancient "Centre of the World" will reassert its hold!

Frankly, I am a little tired of examining everything in terms of power relationships. It's tedious always having to seek out the victim and the victimizer, as if who's on top and who's below is all we need to know. Our challenge now is to *make real* the "post" in "post-colonial," "post-modern," "post-racial," "post-gender," "post-national" (and whatever "posts" that are trending!) As natural members of the Great Assembly of Beings, shouldn't people and other critters be able "to freely come and freely go" across any of the old borders arbitrarily imposed upon the bioregions we inhabit? We need greeters and well-wishers, not militarized personnel policing checkpoints and causing so much grief. In the long run, an eco-friendly etiquette would be more helpful than quotas and exclusionary laws in responding to migratory flux and flow[2]. This is not as Pollyanna-ish as it may sound. Believers and non-believers alike wash their hands and feet before entering a temple or mosque; family and guests automatically slip out of their shoes before stepping onto a tatami mat. And no enforcers are required! Sure, it may seem a little inconvenient if you're in a rush, but who wants to muddy the floor where you pray or foul the nest where you eat and take your rest? Such sensible customs rooted in respect for the Self and our surroundings (unlike the paranoid Customs in airports) make the transition from one zone to another a little special, even up-lifting.

Have no fear, there is no crisis at the border that xxxxxxxx xxxxxxx xxxxxx has crossed over. It's not like there are going to be entire caravans of English-speaking poets wanting to become Translated-Chinese poets. When you come down to it, have you ever heard of any other poet who has suffered from his particular species of L.I.D.—Literary Identity Disorder? Think how frustrated xxxxxxxx xxxxxxx xxxxxx must be. Inside he feels like a Chinese poet, but he knows he will never be recognized as one if he cannot get the Chinese literary establishment to find a place for him in its canon. His desire to reify his true identity is no doubt inscrutable for the majority of us who have never felt the slightest bit of distress regarding the identities that we inherit from the circumstances of our birth and upbringing. If you were born and raised in America, lived there as an adult, and only wrote in English, then of course you would take for granted that you were an American poet. Nothing out of order in that picture!

Try, though, to imagine the inner state of the writer who looks and sounds just like you but deep-down senses that he belongs to a different poetic tradition, even though—amazingly enough— he can neither read nor write its language. Transitioning for him would seem to be much simpler (and less costly) than fixing G.I.D.—just learn Chinese! Poor xxxxxxxx xxxxxxx xxxxxx, whether he is linguistically challenged or simply too lazy, you can tell from the correspondence that he is still suffering from a radical disjunction between his nominal identity as an American poet and his innate affinity with the poetic sensibility of Chinese literati. You may think he has trapped himself in a ridiculous binary struggle and that his inner Chinese self is not for real but go back and reread his poems. How telling it is when xxxxxxxx xxxxxxx xxxxxx wants to honor his brother's eightieth birthday he draws upon Su Tung-po's beautiful little poem about the empty swing; or when he sits next to the stream in the *Garden of Flowing Fragrance*, he remembers Chuang Tzu walking by a river with his fellow philosopher Hui Tzu; even when he contemplates his relationship to local wildlife in his neighboring arroyo, he calls our attention to the Taoist principle of "non-action." I can go on—

every night he sleeps next to a scroll-painting of a crab-eating monkey; he transforms the sound of leaf-blowers on his back porch into temple wind-chimes, finds hope in a Ming Dynasty Buddha submerged in the Hongmen Gorges and courage in Meng Chiao's bitter-throbbing "Heart Songs." Is it any wonder he was inspired to strike up a relationship with the figures he believes represent the tradition of Chinese poetry? It has been said of Arthur Waley that he had no interest in going to Modern China when he could happily live in the Tang Dynasty through the literature he loved. Thanks to translators like Waley, xxxxxxxx xxxxxxx xxxxx can also feel at home in Ancient China, without even reading or   speaking Chinese!

I confess I am not exactly sure what my friend had envisioned when he asked me to provide textual commentary. I am happy to root for his success, but I suspect the questions I have raised about the origin of the letters and their transmission through that shadowy figure *J' Han-shan* will strike him as entirely unnecessary. It would be just like him to say— "Forget your opining, stick to the facts—add more notes about all the stuff the reader should know, like literary allusions and historical references." Well, of course, if I wanted to follow in the same indulgent foot (noting) steps as Charles Kinbote and David Foster Wallace, I could double the length of "Correspondence with The Immortals," make my commentary as wildly absurd as the "Commentary" of

Pale Fire, pile obscurity upon obscurity in a maddeningly small font as in Infinite Jest. Call me "Nipat's Lippitt," if you like, but I prefer to let the letters and the poems of this book speak for themselves and not give free rein to my obsessive-compulsive nature. Besides, in our new Age of Sedentary Self-Service, the relationship between scholars and the public has changed. With so much information readily available at the tips of your fingers, you are now empowered, Dear Reader, to do your own sleuthing in xxxxxxxx xxxxxxx xxxxxx's Garden of Flowing Fragrance. In time, even from your couch, you will be able to pick up its subtle scents and trace back to the branch "the blossoms that blow," as Kung once said, "from the east to the west."

—J. L. Brewer, Retired Foreign Lecturer of Literature, Nara Women's University

Endnotes

1   On second thought, I am actually a little proud that Georgie first began talking in her "sleep" when she and her Irish husband were visiting our own "Golden Land." As Yeats explains in A Vision, "We had one of those little sleeping compartments in a train, with two berths, and were somewhere in Southern California." Not only were they on C.P. Huntington's Southern Pacific Line but they were traveling either to or from Pasadena-San Marino where they stayed for three days. That was in the same auspicious year Myron Hunt designed Henry Huntington's library. If they had come three years later in 1922, they surely would have met the former Theosophical avatar, Krishnamurti, who had just settled in the Ojai Valley near Santa Barbara. At that time before its roads were paved, this lovely healing-spot was as secluded as "Peach Blossom Spring." Indeed, Krishnamurti once told a friend, "If I had nowhere to go in the world, I would come to Ojai. I would sit under an orange tree; it would shade me from the sun, and I could live on the fruit." I am sure this pronouncement would strike a deep chord with my friend yyyyyyy yyyyyy yyyyy who likes to boast that his maternal grandmother, a lapsed Catholic, turned to Oriental philosophy in the middle of her life's journey. Carrying on the torch, his mother and father conceived

him in the Ojai Valley Inn. There you have it, ab ovo, his spiritual pedigree, which I know first-hand from our shared zip code is solidly upper (not lower) middle class!

2   Here's a rule of thumb for bioregional inhabitant-ship: know the fauna and flora of your watershed—who eats what and whom; study carrying capacity; maintain the commons; don't go crazy weeding out and cutting down; raise up your eyes to the sun, moon, and stars; "teach the children about the cycles." As for Dreamers, if like Walt Whitman you can "invite your soul to lean and loaf at your ease and observe a spear of summer grass," you're home free.

—J.L.B.

Acknowledgements

As I note in "The First Letter," I have been reading Chinese poetry in English since I was a teenager. A complete list of the writers I am indebted to is impossible to pin down, but I would like to give a shout-out to these translators and their books: Ezra Pound, *Cathay and Confucius—The Unwobbling Pivot,The Great Digest, The Analects;* Witter Bynner, *The Jade Mountain: A Chinese Anthology;* Arthur Waley, *The Book of Songs;* Paul Reps and Nyogen Senzaki, *Zen Flesh-Zen Bones;* Gary Snyder, *Cold Mountain Poems of Han Shan;* Cyril Birch (with Donald Keene), *Anthology of Chinese Literature, Vols. 1&2;* Thomas Merton, *The Way of ChuangTzu;* Tony Barnstone, Willis Barnstone, & Xu Haixin, *Laughing Lost in The Mountains—Poems of Wang Wei;* Burton Watson, *Su Tung-p'o: Selections from a Sung Dynasty Poet;* Stephen Addiss & Stanley Lombardo, *Tao Teh Ching;* David Hinton, *The Selected Poems of Po Chü-I, The Late Poems of Meng Chiao,* and the anthology, *Classical Chinese Poetry;* Stephen Owen, *Readings in Chinese Literary Thought.*

—x.x.x.

About the Editor

Jonathan Lippitt Brewer was born in Los Angeles in 1948. He is a graduate of St. John's College, Santa Fe, N.M. (B.A., Liberal Arts) and the University of California, Berkeley (M.A., Ph.D., English Literature). He has studied with the poets Charles Bell, Arnold Weinstein, John Anson, Robert Pinsky, and Peter Dale Scott. In 1971, he became a conscientious objector and fulfilled his alternate service by teaching English in northern Thailand. He later lived in India and spent time in and out of ashrams, until he entered graduate school and wrote a dissertation on Eastern meditative practice in the poetry of Yeats, Pound, and Snyder. In 1996, he went to Japan as a tourist, stayed-on as a part-time teacher at several colleges and universities in Kyoto, and eventually became a Foreign Lecturer of English & American Literature at two national universities— Nara Women's University (2004—2012) and Kyushu University (2013-2015). He currently lives in Sacramento, CA.

About Kingston University Press

Kingston University Press has been publishing high-quality commercial and academic titles for more than ten years.

KUP's mission is to publish voices that reflect and appeal to our community at the university as well as the wider reading community of readers and writers in the UK and beyond.

Since 2015 all the books we have published have been produced by students on the MA Publishing and BA Publishing courses, working with authors from within our academic community and collaborative partners from the wider Kingston community.

@KU_press

This book was edited, designed, typeset and produced by students on the MA Publishing course at Kingston University, London.

To find out more about our hands-on, professionally focused and flexible MA and BA programmes please visit:

www.kingston.ac.uk
www.kingstonpublishing.wordpress.com
@kingstonjourno

www.ingramcontent.com/pod-product-compliance
Lightning Source LLC
Chambersburg PA
CBHW020938090426

42736CB00010B/1186